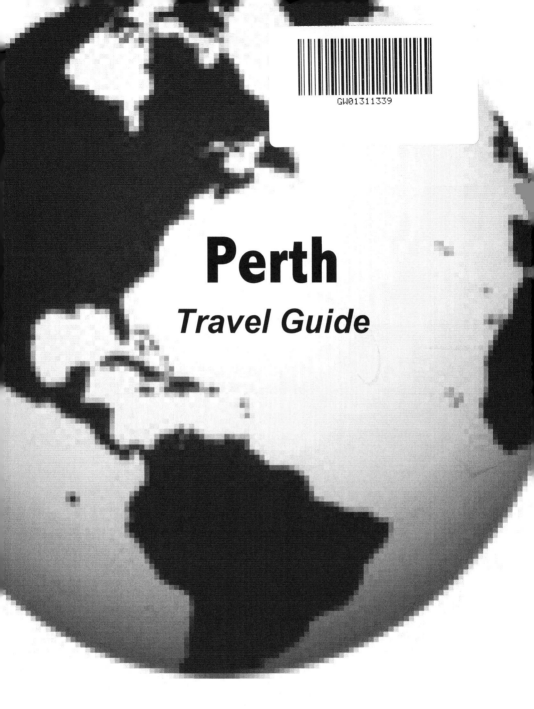

Perth
Travel Guide

Quick Trips Series

No part of this publication may be reproduced, stored in a retrieval system, or transmitted, in any form or by any means without the prior written permission of the publisher, nor be otherwise circulated in any form of binding or cover other than that in which it is published and without similar condition being imposed on the subsequent purchaser. If there are any errors or omissions in copyright acknowledgements the publisher will be pleased to insert the appropriate acknowledgement in any subsequent printing of this publication. Although we have taken all reasonable care in researching this book we make no warranty about the accuracy or completeness of its content and disclaim all liability arising from its use.

Copyright © 2016, Astute Press
All Rights Reserved.

Table of Contents

PERTH   5
- Customs & Culture 8
- Geography 10
- Climate 14

SIGHTS & ACTIVITIES: WHAT TO SEE & DO   17
- Western Australian Museum 17
- Scitech Museum 20
- Rottnest Island 22
- York 26
- Fremantle 29
- Crown Perth & Burswood Entertainment Complex 32
- Margaret River Wine Region 34
- Cottesloe Beach 36
- Kings Park 37
- Swan Bell Tower 39

BUDGET TIPS   43
- Accommodation 43

Kangaroo Inn	43
The Royal Hotel	44
City Waters	45
The Witchs Hat	45
Goodearth Hotel East Perth	46

PLACES TO EAT 47

Friends Restaurant	47
Opus Restaurant	48
Canton Bay Chinese	49
Zephyr Mediterranean Cuisine	50
Cantina 663	51

SHOPPING 52

Garden City Shopping Center	52
Coventry Square Market	52
Hay Street Mall	53
Harbor Town Perth	53
Carillon City	54

KNOW BEFORE YOU GO   55

ENTRY REQUIREMENTS	55
HEALTH INSURANCE	55
TRAVELLING WITH PETS	56
AIRPORTS	58
AIRLINES	59
HUBS	61
MONEY MATTERS	62
CURRENCY	62
BANKING/ATMS	62
CREDIT CARDS	63
TOURIST TAX	64
CLAIMING BACK VAT	64

- Tipping Policy 65
- Connectivity 65
  - Mobile Phones 65
- Dialling Code 66
- Emergency Numbers 67
- General Information 67
- Public Holidays 67
- Time Zones 68
- Daylight Savings Time 68
- School Holidays 69
- Trading Hours 69
- Driving Policy 70
- Drinking Policy 71
- Smoking Policy 71
- Electricity 72
- Food & Drink 72
- Useful Websites 74

PERTH TRAVEL GUIDE

Perth

Set on the tranquil waters of the Swan River is Perth, the capital city of Western Australia. 20 kilometers inland from the Indian Ocean on the one side and the Darling Scarp range on the other, Perth provides its visitors with a wonderful mix of nature and modernity that has captured the imagination of an increasing number of tourists in recent years. The modern infrastructure coupled with the

PERTH TRAVEL GUIDE

warm, moderate climate helps to attract 3.5 million visitors every year.

Originally founded by British Admiral James Stirling in 1829, the city of Perth got its official city status in 1856. It was named after the Scottish city of Perth, influenced by the Scottish soldier and politician Sir George Murray, who was born in Perth, Scotland. Perth (Australia) grew in prominence and population during the 19th century gold rush. It was a major naval base of the US Navy during World War II. In the later decades, Perth stayed in prominence for its mining operations as well as its many oil and gas fields – contributing to 90% of the state's exports.

The influx of immigrants, especially from Britain, Italy, Greece, and the Slavic countries brought about a mix of

PERTH TRAVEL GUIDE

culture and communities in Perth. The city today is divided into 7 districts. The Perth City district is the commercial and shopping center with numerous skyscrapers and branded stores dotting the metropolitan area. Cutting right through the heart of this district is the arterial St George's Terrace, lined with early 20th century residences of the clergies and clerks of St George's Cathedral along with a number of the tallest skyscrapers of Perth. The street is a must visit for any tourist in Perth for its eclectic mix of the old charm and the nouveau glamour.

The Fremantle and Northbridge districts are popular for entertainment and nightlife attracting many tourists. The Northern Suburbs and Southern Suburbs are prime residential areas. The Coast district attracts the beach lovers and is also the perfect place for a romantic

PERTH TRAVEL GUIDE

getaway with its beautiful sunsets. The Hills district is the one for nature lovers, with beautiful scenic drives, numerous vineyards, and the John Forest National Park.

This once-isolated city is now the fastest growing in the country. Its diverse population brings forth a great mix of culture, cuisine, and lifestyle. From beautiful beaches to magnificent vineyards, and from stunning architecture to a vibrant nightlife, Perth offers a wide range of activities and attractions for visitors of every age and interest.

🌐 Customs & Culture

Perth is a metropolitan city with more than half its population having a foreign ancestry. British, Irish, Italian, Scottish, and Chinese account for more than half its population. The foreign influence is evident in many

PERTH TRAVEL GUIDE

pockets of the city like the numerous Italian eateries in the Fremantle area and the Chinatown in Northbridge.

The city of Perth has a vibrant art and culture scene. There are many performance venues all over the city with the most popular being the Perth Cultural Centre that is home to a number of museums, galleries, and theaters. Music lovers can head to the West Australian Opera or the West Australia Ballet. Perth is also home to many rock and pop bands that perform in open-air and closed venues like the Perth Arena and the Kings Park.

The Western Australia Academy of Performing Arts, Riverside Theatre, the 103-year old His Majesty's Theatre, and the Regal Theatre are popular venues that have cradled the careers of many successful broadcasters and actors.

PERTH TRAVEL GUIDE

The city has a number of popular annual events. The Fringe World Festival and the Perth International Arts Festival between January and March are 2 of the most popular events of the city. Whereas the first attracts over 800 comedians performing in over 150 shows across various venues in the city, the latter is the oldest arts festival in the southern hemisphere featuring numerous concerts, plays, films, and dance events in a month-long celebration of the performing arts.

The pyrotechnic display on Australia (national) Day in the Skyworks festival every January is flocked by thousands of locals and visitors alike. Food lovers can attend the Eat Drink Perth food festival in March or the Good Food and Wine Show in June that not only celebrates the locally made wine, cheese, and chocolates, but also hold

PERTH TRAVEL GUIDE

cooking classes and organize culinary feasts. The week-long Perth Royal Show in September is a spectacle with carnival rides, free live entertainment, crafts fair, and fireworks display.

🌐 Geography

The city of Perth is the most isolated city in Australia and the 2nd most isolated capital city in the world (after Honolulu, Hawaii), with the closest major Australian city, Adelaide at a distance of 2129 km! In spite of this distinction, Perth is very well connected by air, land, and water.

Perth is served by the Perth Airport (IATA: PER) - http://www.perthairport.com.au. The same airport has the domestic and international terminal albeit on opposite sides of the runway which is a distance of 9 km by road.

PERTH TRAVEL GUIDE

Located about 20 min from the Perth City, the airport has 4 terminals with T1 as the international terminal. The airport has direct connections with a number of cities in South Africa, England, Malaysia, and Thailand.

From the airport, one can choose from a number of transport options to enter the city. The 24-hr service of the Airport CONNECT Shuttle - http://www.perthairportconnect.com.au/ is one of the cheapest costing $15 (Australian dollars) for the one-way ride. There are 5 drop off points in the city to choose from. Public buses run by TransPerth connect T3 and T4 to the Kings Park in the city. Details of the schedule can be found at - http://www.transperth.wa.gov.au/. Taxis, available outside the terminals, cost about $40 to the city center ($60 to Fremantle) and are quicker than the shuttle. It is a better option than the shuttle for a group of

PERTH TRAVEL GUIDE

2 or 3 people. Rental cars are also available with many of the popular global brands offering their services, including Avis, Hertz, and Budget.

The trans-continental India Pacific rail service connects Perth to Sydney via Adelaide in a ride that is listed as one of the world's greatest train journeys. In the 3-nights-4-days journey, the train passes through some exquisitely picturesque sceneries as well as the 478 km long Nullarbor Plain – the world's longest stretch of straight railway track!

The well-maintained highways do make traveling by road an option, but the distance is often over whelming to many people. Greyhound Australia - http://www.greyhound.com.au/ has multiple connections to different Australian cities to and from Perth. Multiple

PERTH TRAVEL GUIDE

options are also available with Transwa - http://www.transwa.wa.gov.au/.

Perth features in the itineraries of many cruise tours of the Australian coast during the summer months – November to February. Although it is not the cheapest way to get to Perth, it certainly gives the option to explore the beautiful waters of the Indian Ocean.

Once in the city, visitors can enjoy the free public bus service run by TransPerth connecting Fremantle, Perth City, Northbridge, and Joondalup. These buses run on 3 routes in the Central Area Transit (CAT) Zone connecting most of the city attractions.

The metropolitan zone of the city has 5 train lines with terminals at Perth CBD, Fremantle, Joondalup, Midland,

PERTH TRAVEL GUIDE

and Mandurah. All the major train stations also have a connecting public bus services. Details can be found in the TransPerth website.

Taxis are available all over town and one may flag down a taxi or use the call-taxi service. Operators include Swan Taxis (Tel: 13 13 30) and Black and White Taxis (Tel: 13 10 08). Due to government regulations all dispatch companies have the same rate. The base fare is $3.90 ($5.70 on weekends) with an increment of $1.59 per km. It is customary to tip the driver a dollar or two.

Perth has excellent facilities for the healthy and eco-friendly options of seeing the city on foot or on bicycle. Some of the attractions can be easily explored on foot like Fremantle and the city center. Cycling is also a great option to see Perth. Details of the routes and facilities can

PERTH TRAVEL GUIDE

be found at -

http://www.transport.wa.gov.au/activetransport/24022.asp
.

Ferries are a common mode of transport on the River Swan.. Fremantle, South Perth, and Rottnest Island are a few of the places that are connected by regular high-speed ferry services.

For those planning to drive, it has to be kept in mind that Australia has a left-lane driving rule. Speed limits are 110 km per hr for highways and 50 km per hr for built-up areas. Speed limits are strictly enforced and driving even 5 km above the speed limit will incur a fine. To drive in Australia, one must be 21 years of age and have an International Driver's License in English.

PERTH TRAVEL GUIDE

 Climate

Perth has a Mediterranean climate with hot and dry summers and wet and cool winters. Being in the southern hemisphere, summer months are from December to March with February being the hottest. The average high in the summer months is around 32 degrees Celsius and low around 18 degrees.

Winter settles between May and September with the average high around 19 degrees Celsius and the low around 8 degrees. June and July are the wettest months with rainfall over 150 mm. With 3200 hrs of annual sunshine, it is the sunniest Australian city attracting tourists all the year round with the peak in the summer months.

PERTH TRAVEL GUIDE

PERTH TRAVEL GUIDE

Sights & Activities: What to See & Do

🌐 Western Australian Museum

Perth Cultural Centre

James Street, Perth

WA 6000

Tel: +61 08 9212 3700

http://museum.wa.gov.au/

Originally opened as the Geological Museum in 1891, it was transformed to the Western Australian Museum and Art Gallery in 1897.

The present museum in Perth is partly housed in the Old Gaol, one of the oldest standing buildings in WA.

PERTH TRAVEL GUIDE

The Western Australian Museum is established under the Museum Act of 1969 and has over 4.7 million items in its collection in Archeology, Anthropology, Zoology, and Earth and Planetary Sciences. There are 6 main sites of the museum in the metropolitan zone and the regional zone. Sites in the metropolitan zone include Perth, Maritime, and Shipwreck Galleries. The regional sites are in Albany, Geralton, and Calgary Boulder.

The Perth site is near the Perth Train Station and is accessible through the free Blue CAT bus. The museum hosts many major exhibitions that attract hundreds of thousands of visitors every year. The permanent exhibitions include the Diamonds to Dinosaurs – an exhibition that explores 12 billion years of history and features rock specimens of celestial objects and dinosaur skeleton casts. The Katta Dinjoong exhibition explores the

PERTH TRAVEL GUIDE

culture and history of Western Australia's aboriginal people. The Museum is open from 9:30 am to 5:00 pm and has free admission but a $5 donation is suggested. It is closed on Christmas Day, Boxing Day, New Year's Day, and Good Friday.

The WA Maritime Museum site is at the Victoria Quay in Fremantle (Tel: +61 08 9431 8334). It reflects the city's affinity to the ocean and its history as a port city. The museum has a number of sailing boats and leisure boats in its collections, including the America's Cup winning Australia II yacht. Other featured collections include the HMAS Ovens submarine, and the famous Parry Endeavour vessel. Its opening hours are the same as the Perth site. The museum has an entry fee: Adult - $10, Child (5 – 15yrs) - $3. A similar amount is charged for entry into the submarine Ovens. Combined tickets at $16

PERTH TRAVEL GUIDE

are also available. Family and students discounts are available.

Located close to the Maritime Museum is the Shipwreck Galleries at Cliff Street in Fremantle (Tel: 9431 8469). It is close to the Fremantle Station and is accessible by the free CAT – Stop 23. This 2 level museum is regarded as one of the foremost maritime archeology museums in the southern hemisphere. It is housed in a refurbished mid 19th century Commissariat building and has in its collections numerous ships that were wrecked along the WA coastline. Interesting collections include the original timbers from the early 17th century wreck of the Batavia, and many artifacts from a number of Dutch shipwrecks. The Galleries have free entry but a $5 donation is suggested.

PERTH TRAVEL GUIDE

The regional museums are located far from the Perth City and have similar collections albeit much less in number. These museums are also involved with community development and workshops.

The WA Museum has an online store where can buy a variety of interesting items including books, DVDs, jewelry, and ship prints.

Scitech Museum

Sutherland Street

West Perth

WA 6005

Tel: +61 08 9215 0700

http://www.scitech.org.au/

Opened in 1988, the Scitech Museum is a non-profit

PERTH TRAVEL GUIDE

organization that operates a Discovery Centre, a planetarium, and an interactive science museum. The primary aim of this organization is to increase the interest and awareness in technology, science, and mathematics. Although the workshops, exhibits, and activities in Scitech are aimed towards children up to 12 years of age, the organization has been able to attract adults of all ages.

A great place for the whole family, Scitech has a number of exhibitions throughout the year. Scitech includes the Discoverland (for toddlers between 3 to 7 years of age), CSIRO Lab which exhibits the everyday use of science in our lives, the Horizon Planetarium (to reopen in late 2013 after going through a multimillion dollar refurbishment), the Puppet Theatre, the multimedia digital studio, and the Science Theatre. There is also the Discovery Shop with

PERTH TRAVEL GUIDE

its wide variety of science gadgets, gifts, and modeling kits.

Scitech is open from 10:00 am until 5:00 pm on weekends, school holidays, and public holidays. It is open from 9:30 am until 4:00 pm on weekdays. It is closed only on Christmas Day and Boxing Day (Dec 26). Entry ticket to Scitech: Adult - $17; Child (4 to 15 yrs) - $11. Children below 3 years of age have free entry. Group discounts are available.

🌍 Rottnest Island

Located 20 km off the coast of Perth, Rottnest Island – locally known as Rotto – is a popular getaway for the visitors and locals of Perth. It was originally inhabited by the aboriginal people and was located by Dutch and British sailors in the 17th century. The island, with a land

PERTH TRAVEL GUIDE

area of about 19 sq km, is an A Class Reserve and is controlled entirely by the WA government and does not allow any private ownership.

The island can be reached easily by using any of the ferry services offered by Rottnest Express - http://www.rottnestexpress.com.au/, Rottnest Fast Ferries - http://www.rottnestfastferries.com.au/, and Oceanic Cruises - http://www.oceaniccruises.com.au/whalewatching.aspx (they also have cruises for whale watching). Ferry ports are at Fremantle (B-Shed and Northport) and Perth (Barrack St). One-way ticket costs about $30, but there is an additional $17 government fee.

Once on the island, the best way to see it is by cycling. One can rent bicycles for as low as $30 for the day.

PERTH TRAVEL GUIDE

There are no cars on the island, but one can buy a day ticket for the public bus service.

The island was used as a colonial settlement for a brief period of time. Inhabited by the aboriginals, it was also used as a prison. It served as a naval and military base during both the World Wars. Between the 2 Wars, and since then, the island has been a popular recreation spot. The aboriginal, military, maritime, and colonial history can be explored through many museums and guided tours on the island.

A popular attraction is the 1857 Rottnest Museum in Digby Drive. Housed in a refurbished granary and hayshed, it was built by Aboriginal prisoners. It houses an interesting collection of marine wrecks, and items of natural history and items of the prisoners on the island.

PERTH TRAVEL GUIDE

Some of the displays are also exhibited in the Thomson Bay pilot boathouse. The museum has free entry. Other museums on the island include the Salt Store Gallery and the historic Lamas Cottage.

There are a number of tours of the island. The popular ones include the 2-hr Discovery Tour (Adult $35; Child $17) which is a full commentary coach tour that starts from the main bus stop. It explores the history, culture, wildlife, and heritage of the island. The Oliver Hill Gun and Tunnel Tour explores the guns and tunnels on the island from the two World Wars. The Wadjemup Lighthouse Tours (Adult $8; Child $3.50) are between 11:00 am and 2:30 pm and gives the visitor an opportunity to have a 360 degree view of the stunning land and waterscape surrounding the island.

PERTH TRAVEL GUIDE

The 90 minute Rottnest Adventure Tour between September and June explores the full coastline of the island. A hi-speed boat circum-navigates the island offering interesting information on bays, wildlife, and secluded beaches. Rotto also has segway, bicycle and walking tours.

The Rottnest Island is an attraction in itself with is beautiful coastline and scenic views. The beaches of the island were awarded the prestigious 'Explore Australia 2007' award. Rotto has 63 secluded beaches and 20 bays to choose from. Some of the popular ones include the Fish Hook Bay, Cape Vlamingh, Geordie Bay, and Salmon Bay. Fishing is very popular in Rotto, one can even buy the angling items on the island. For water adventure lovers, there are facilities for surfing, diving, and snorkeling.

PERTH TRAVEL GUIDE

Nature lovers can head to the daisy fields or go for bottle-nosed dolphin spotting in the Salmon Bay. The endemic quokka marsupial, marbled gecko, motorbike frog (Western green tree frog), pelicans, and stingrays make animal and fish spotting an unforgettable experience.

The Rottnest Island is perfect for great day out for the whole family. The Family Fun Park, Mini Putt-Putt, and Aqua Park have facilities for family games, mini-golf, trampolines, and rock climbing. There is also a 9-hole golf course.

Rotto has a number of cafés, restaurants, and bars sprinkled all over the island. Popular among those are the Aristos Waterfront seafood café, Governors Sports Bar, Dome Rottnest European café, and the Rottnest Bakery.

PERTH TRAVEL GUIDE

 York

Located about 96 km east of Perth, the town of York is the first and oldest surviving inland settlement of the state of Western Australia. This small town was founded in 1831 in the fertile Avon Valley, 2 years after the founding of Perth, and presently has a population of less than 2500, making it a perfect place to visit for a quiet and relaxing day-out.

The best way to see the town is by foot. The picturesque streets and buildings retain the heritage charm of Perth's favorite weekend escape. Named after the English city of York, the Australian namesake has a number of Federation and Victorian buildings. In fact, it is one of the few Australian towns with a status of 'Historic Town'. Originally built for farming and mining needs, York was a busy town by the late 19th century. Along with a number of

PERTH TRAVEL GUIDE

mills, the town also saw a growth of administrative buildings and churches during this period. The Courthouse, Imperial Hotel, Police Station, Post and Telegraph Office, railway station buildings, York Hospital, York Roller Flower Mill, and the St Patrick's Church were particularly impressive.

York has transformed itself from a farming town to a favorite tourist spot in WA. There are a number of attractions in town. The York Town Hall has been transformed into the Information Center (Tel: 3641 1301) where one can pick a free map and get an update of the attractions in town. The Avon Park in Lowe Street by the River Avon is a favorite picnic spot. Gwambygine Park on the southern highway has York's oldest homestead and a viewing tower very close to the river.

PERTH TRAVEL GUIDE

With free gas barbeques, picnic tables, and a kid's area, it is another favorite picnic spot for the family. The mid 19th century Courthouse and Gaol is open from Thursday to Monday (10:00 am – 4:00 pm) between March and December. Originally a convicts' depot, the Residency Museum provides a great insight to the history of the region. The York Motor Museum in Avon Terrace has an interesting collection of vintage classic, veteran, and racing cars. Also in Avon Terrace are the sandalwood yards where sandalwood – one of the major exports - was brought in after the felling.

Adventure lovers can head to Mount Brown Lookout for a panoramic view of the city at 342m above sea level. The Skydive Express on Spencer's Brook Road is a multi award winning skydiving facility. The Swing Bridge on

PERTH TRAVEL GUIDE

Lowe Street, built by the convicts, was the first temporary bridge in the town.

For those looking to buy gifts, there is the Sock Factory or the York Mill Gallery. The Sock Factory on Stephen Street is the last existing manufacturer of socks in the state! They also sell a variety of products including ugg boots, scarves, and olive oil. The historic York Mill Gallery in Broom Street has crafts and souvenirs for sale. It also sells artwork and hosts free monthly exhibitions.

🌏 Fremantle

Located 30 minutes away from the Perth city center, the neighboring town of Fremantle – or Freo to the locals – is the oldest port town of Western Australia and the state's gateway to the west.

PERTH TRAVEL GUIDE

One can get to Fremantle by taking the TransPerth bus (line 98 or 99) or any of the commuter trains from the Perth Train Station. Although short, the journey is breathtaking as one passes the beaches, ocean and the port area. Once in the city, there are free CAT buses every 10 minutes. One can also walk through a major part of the city.

Fremantle has a number of attractions, the most popular being the Western Australian Museum and the Shipwreck Galleries (discussed separately in this section). The mid 19th century Fremantle Prison - http://www.fremantleprison.com.au - is a World Heritage building that served as the major maximum-security prison of the state until 1991 when it was closed and transformed into a museum, an art gallery, and a conference center. It has a number of intriguing and

PERTH TRAVEL GUIDE

interesting tours including the Doing Time Tour ($19, 30 min) – a tour of the prison including the gallows and the solitary cells; the Great Escape Tour ($19, 75 min) – a tour exploring the various attempts made by prisoners to escape from this prison and a visit to the escape-proof cell. The Tunnels Tour ($60, 2 hr 30 min) goes 20m underground to the blast holes and submerged passageways that are only accessible by boat.

This tour must be pre-booked over the phone only (Tel: +61 08 9336 9200). The scary Torchlight Tours ($25, 90 min) are held ever Wednesday and Friday evenings from 6:30 pm onwards and explores the solitary confinements and the morgues. It is not recommended for children bellow 10 and people with heart problems. Entry to the Gatehouse, the prison gallery, gift shop, and the aptly named Prison Café is free.

PERTH TRAVEL GUIDE

The early 19th century 12-sided Round House - http://www.fremantleroundhouse.com.au/ - at Arthur Head is another prison turned museum. It is housed in the oldest public building of the state. A major attraction is the firing of the cannon from the Signal Station everyday at 1:00 pm; a lucky member from the public is chosen to trigger the shot! Below the Round House is the Whaler's Tunnel built in 1937 by the Fremantle Whaling Company to gain easy access between the city and the Bathers Beach.

A walk through the century-old Fishing Boat Harbor or the streets of Fremantle will take one past many colonial architecture and heritage pubs. The century-old Fremantle markets are a great place to buy local products. One can also spend a casual evening trying

PERTH TRAVEL GUIDE

some local seafood, freshly-brewed ale or premium wine. After doing some whale-spotting, Fremantle is the perfect place to watch the sunset in the Indian Ocean.

The city is a treat for the shopaholics with many galleries of Aboriginal art, curios, as well as high street fashion stores. Music lovers can head to the Newport Club, the Metropolis Fremantle, or the Kulcha Club above the Dome Café.

Crown Perth & Burswood Entertainment Complex

Bolton Avenue

Burswood, Perth

WA 6100

Tel: +61 08 9362 7777

http://www.crownperth.com.au/

PERTH TRAVEL GUIDE

Located across the Swan River from the central business district (CBD) of Perth is the southeastern suburb of Burswood with the popular Burswood Entertainment Complex that was renamed as the Crown Perth in 2011 after it was taken over by the Crown Limited Company. The huge complex has a 24-hr casino, a 2300-seat theater, a 20000-seat arena, 2 luxury hotels, a convention center, a nightclub, and over 2 dozen restaurants and bars! The complex is served by the Burswood Railway Station that links it to the Perth CBD.

The complex was built in the mid-1980s by businessman Dallas Dempster. The first to be built was the casino followed by a hotel, golf course, amphitheater, and tennis courts. It was rebranded after being bought by James

PERTH TRAVEL GUIDE

Packer, son of the legendary Australian media mogul Kerry Packer, who owned the Crown Limited.

The highlight of the complex is the 24-hr casino – in other words, a casino that never closes! The casino is packed with 1500 slot machines, 2500 poker machines, and over 300 gaming tables.

The Casino is divided into many rooms namely the Pearl Room, Meridian Room, and Riviera Room. The theater at Crown Perth hosts a number of performances throughout the year that ranges from plays, major concerts to world famous musicals. The hotels include the 5-star Crown Metropol and the 4-star Crown Promenade.

Even if one is not planning to stay in any of the hotels or gamble at the casino, the Crown Perth is worth a visit for its vibrancy, glamour, and its range of offerings. It is the one-stop spot for those who are looking to splurge.

🌐 Margaret River Wine Region

With 5500 hectares of vineyards and over 215 wineries with 'crushings' amounting to thousands of tons every year, the Margaret River region is made up of numerous boutique-sized wine producers. A Mediterranean maritime climate and mean annual temperature fluctuation of only 7.6 degrees Celsius makes this region the best suited in the whole country for wine production, accounting for over 20% percent of Australia's premium wine market.

The primary types of wine produced from the region are Sauvignon Blanc, Cabernet Sauvignon, Riesling, Chardonnay, Merlot, Petit Verdot, Shiraz, Semillion, and Cabernet Franc.

PERTH TRAVEL GUIDE

As there are many wineries in the region it is a good idea to visit the Margaret River Visitor Center (100 Bussell Highway; Tel: +61 08 9780 5911) to get an update on the wineries, tours, and other attractions of the region.

One of the most popular is the multi-award winning Bushtucker River and Wine Tours run by award winning guide Helen Lee. There are separate tours for the winery, brewery, and the river, and one can enjoy over 40 tastings and even get to paddle on the Margaret River.

A popular winery is the Knee Deep Wines - http://kneedeepwines.com.au/. The winery has a restaurant, a physical and an online store. This multi-award winning winery is also a popular venue for weddings. It is open 10:00 am to 5:00 pm every day; closed on Christmas Day and Good Friday.

The Margaret River region is not only famous for the vineyards; it is also home to many natural wonders, the most popular being the limestone caves in Forest Grove. The cave – known as Lake Cave – is located below the CaveWorks (Tel: +61 08 9757 7411) on Caves Road. The 'mirrored wonderland' is one of the most active caves in the country and has tons of stalactites hanging from the roof of the cave.

🌎 Cottesloe Beach

The picturesque Cottesloe Beach is located in the Town of Cottesloe, a beachside suburb of Perth. The secluded beach with calm turquoise waters reflects the tranquility and beauty of nature. The beach was named amongst the

PERTH TRAVEL GUIDE

best in the world among family beaches in 2009 by Lonely Planet.

Locally known as the Cott, the beach is easily accessible from the Perth center by road and rail. It is connected by the TransPerth buses and commuter trains which stop at the Cottesloe Station, barely 600m from the beach.

The beach is popular with the locals and visitors alike for snorkeling, surfing, and swimming. One can also have a relaxed glass of beer or wine with the beautiful Indian Ocean sunset at the horizon. The white-sand beaches are with the shady pine trees is ideal for a family day out. While the crystal clear waters are enjoyed by the swimmers; those interested in snorkeling head to the reefs and rocky shores.

The boulevard of the beach is dotted with cafes, bars, and restaurants open almost throughout the day and late into the night. The place becomes especially busy during the weekends attracting crowds from far and near. In the summer months, the beach is transformed into a gallery with many sand sculptures as part of the 'Sculpture by the Sea'.

🌐 Kings Park

The 4.06 sq km Kings Park is located to the west of the Central Business District of Perth and is one of the most visited attractions in the city. The Park has a number of attractions inside it that includes the Botanical Gardens, a natural bushland, grassed parkland, a tennis club, a reservoir, and the War Memorial. The War Memorial is an obelisk built on Mt Eliza and overlooks the Perth Water. It

PERTH TRAVEL GUIDE

has a flame of remembrance that was inaugurated by Queen Elizabeth II in 2000.

The Memorial is dedicated to the soldiers enlisted in WA who died in World War I and II, the Boer War, Korean War, and the Vietnam War. The Honor Avenues are lined with plaques dedicated to servicemen who died wounded in service. The Fraser Avenue is lined with Lemon Scented Gum Trees honoring various dignitaries. The Bali Memorial is dedicated to the victims who died in the bomb attack in the Indonesian resort town of Bali in 2002. The Edith Cowan Memorial Clock, erected in 1934 to honor the first woman elected to the Australian Parliament is the first civic monument in Australia that was dedicated to a woman.

PERTH TRAVEL GUIDE

The Botanic Garden spreads over 18 hectares inside the Park. It is home to over 25000 plant species and is popular worldwide for its state of the art research facilities. Every September the Kings Park hosts the Kings Park Festival – the largest wildflower exhibition in Australia.

The Park also has the Aboriginal Art gallery. A visit to the gallery is a must not only to enjoy the art but also to have a stunning panoramic view of the Perth CBD.

🌐 Swan Bell Tower

Riverside Drive

Perth

WA 6000

Tel: +61 08 6210 0444

http://www.thebelltower.com.au/

PERTH TRAVEL GUIDE

A unique piece of architecture overlooking the Swan River on the Riverside Drive is the Swan Bell Tower. It is a set of 18 bells inside an 82.5m high copper and glass bell tower making it one of the largest sets of change-ringing bells in the world. Since its opening in 2000, the Swan Bells have been a major tourist attraction with over a million visitors to date.

12 of the 18 bells are of St Martin-in-the-Fields and are from England. There were originally cast in or before the 14th century and were recast by Queen Elizabeth I in the 16th century. It is one of the few existing set of Royal Bells and the only set to have left England. The Bells were donated to WA during the Australian bicentennial celebrations in 1988. The remaining 6 bells were cast in the Whitechapel Bell Foundry in WA. The path to the Tower is surrounded by ceramic tiles that have come from

PERTH TRAVEL GUIDE

the schools of WA bearing the name of each student in the academic year of 1999.

The bells are rung every day (except Wednesday and Friday) between 12 noon and 1:00 pm. Bell handling demonstrations are given to the public between 11:30 am and 12:30 pm on Wednesdays and Fridays – the only one of its kind in the world.

The entry fee to the Tower is: Adult - $14; Child - $9. Concession tickets are available.

PERTH TRAVEL GUIDE

PERTH TRAVEL GUIDE

Budget Tips

 Accommodation

Kangaroo Inn

123 Murray St

Perth

WA 6000

Tel: +61 08 9325 3508

http://www.kangarooinn.com.au/

Located near the Perth Central Business District and close to the Riverside Drive, the Kangaroo Inn is a newly built hostel that was ranked among the top 10 hostels in Australia by Hostelworld. The air-conditioned hostel has parking facilities and offers free Wi-Fi and free Internet access. Other facilities include luggage storage, safe box, laundry services, and a common room with board games.

PERTH TRAVEL GUIDE

There are 6 room arrangements ranging from 6-bed dorms to single rooms. Rates range from $45 to $115.

The Royal Hotel

531 Wellington St

Perth

WA 6000

Tel: +61 08 9338 5100

http://www.royalhotelperth.com.au/

Located at the corner of Wellington St and Williams St, the Royal Hotel is housed in a colonial styled building with a mix of Victorian styled and modern interior. It is close to the city center and gives the visitor a taste of the old world charm with the basic modern facilities. While the single rooms have an attic roof, there are others which are ensuite and even include a microwave. Non-smoking rooms and family rooms are available. It is a sister hotel to the Comfort Inn Wentworth Plaza which is on the same street.

Rooms range from single to deluxe suites and are very tastefully decorated. Room rates start from $90.

City Waters

118 Terrace Road

Perth

WA 6000

Tel: +61 08 9325 1566

http://www.citywaters.com.au

Located by the Swan River, the City Waters is an old-fashioned waterfront motel.

It is only a 15-minute walk from the Perth Railway Station.

It has 58 1-bedroom and 3 2-bedroom ensuite rooms.

There is Wi-Fi, coin operated laundry machines, and free parking. Rooms come with TV, and a kitchenette.

Booking must be done for at least 2 nights. Room rates start from $130.

The Witchs Hat

148 Palmerston St

Northbridge, Perth

WA 6000

Tel: +61 08 9228 4228

http://witchs-hat.com/

The Witchs Hat is a backpacker's hostel housed in an

PERTH TRAVEL GUIDE

1897 building that looks straight out from a fairy tale! It is a short walk from the city centre and is conveniently located close to the Northbridge nightlife scene. There are free lockers, free tea and coffee, and free barbeques available in the hostel. There is also free parking and free Wi-Fi. There is a common room and a terrace.

There is laundry facility and linens and towels are included in the bed rate. Bed rates start from $36.

Goodearth Hotel East Perth

195 Adelaide Terrace

Perth

WA 6004

Tel: +61 08 9492 7777

http://www.goodearthhotel.com.au

PERTH TRAVEL GUIDE

This 3.5 star hotel is located just a block away from the river and is close to the route of the free CAT bus service. It is located close to the Swan Bell Tower. Facilities include free parking, safe deposit box, hair salon, on-site restaurant, laundry facilities, and a 24-hr reception. It is a smoke-free property.

Rooms come with LCD TVs, and free toiletries. There are many categories of rooms with room rates starting from $95 but it can go up to $200 if not booked in advance.

 Places to Eat

Friends Restaurant

Fortescue Center

20 Terrace Road

Perth East

WA 6004

PERTH TRAVEL GUIDE

Tel: +61 08 9221 0885

http://www.friendsrestaurant.com.au/

With an exceptional wine list, award winning cuisine, and great views of the river, the Friends Restaurant is one of the most popular restaurants in the city serving Australian cuisine.

The plush ambience is coupled with live music making it a favorite place for romantic and anniversary dinners. All starters (includes beef, quail, salmon, and one vegetarian dish) are priced at $25. The main courses are prices at $45 and include kangaroo strip loin and beef in red wine sauce. Desserts are priced at $15. One can also have tea or coffee ($6). There is a very comprehensive wine list with prices starting from $6.

PERTH TRAVEL GUIDE

Opus Restaurant

32 Richardson Street

Perth

WA 6005

Tel: +61 08 9217 8880

http://www.opusrestaurant.com.au/

Serving French and International cuisine, the Opus Restaurant offers its guests a brilliant array of mouth watering dishes in a perfectly warm and elegant ambience.

The starters (Spring Vegetable Salad, Braised Chicken in Truffle and Milk Crisps) are priced from $18. The main dishes are priced at $48 and include Chicken breast in mushroom and potato foam, Venison loin in smoked yoghurt, and lamb in ricotta dumplings. The restaurant is closed on Sundays and Mondays.

Canton Bay Chinese

130 Mounts Bay Road

Perth, WA

http://cantonbaychinese.com.au/

This Chinese restaurant is popular for its tasty food, pocket-friendly takeaway menu, and excellent service. One can also order food online for any of the areas listed on the website. The menu includes 'a la carte' as well as set food menus for families. Soups start from $6.80 and main dishes of chicken or seafood start from $22.80. It also serves a wide variety of beer, alcohol, and ciders, even for home-delivery!

PERTH TRAVEL GUIDE

Zephyr Mediterranean Cuisine

111B Flora Terrace

North Beach, Perth

WA 6020

Tel: +61 08 9246 7033

http://www.zephyrmc.com/aboutUs.shtml

Reservations are recommended for this restaurant that serves excellent Mediterranean cuisine by the well-travelled head chef, Lawrence. Entrees are priced about $20 and include dishes like the seafood chowder in creamy soup and beef carpaccio in marinated mushrooms. Main courses of seafood, tiger prawns, or veal are priced about $35. There are smaller dishes for kids and they are also served free ice cream. It is open from Tuesday to Saturday from 5:30 pm until late hours.

Cantina 663

663 Beaufort Street

Mt Lawley, Perth

WA 6050

Tel: +61 08 9370 4883

http://www.cantina663.com/

With dishes made from fresh local organic produce, this European canteen serves a wide variety of Italian, Spanish, and Portuguese cuisine. The eatery is open from breakfast to late hours and offers a wide variety of items to choose from. Breakfast starts from $9. Lunch or dinner would cost about $30 per person.

PERTH TRAVEL GUIDE

🌐 Shopping

Garden City Shopping Center

http://www.gardencity.com.au/

Located to the south of Perth in Booragoon, this mall has valet parking, ATMs, customer lounge, parent facilities, and of course a long list of stores ranging from fashion and beauty to electronics and entertainment. There is a style studio for enhanced personalized shopping and styling. One can also buy fresh produce along with confectioneries. The mall also has the quintessential fast food, restaurants, and cafes.

Coventry Square Market

http://www.coventryvillage.com.au/

PERTH TRAVEL GUIDE

Located close to the Centro Galleria in Morley, the Coventry Village is a popular market with locals and visitors alike. There are over 140 specialty stores in home ware, fashion, gifts, and services. One can also choose from the biggest range of fresh produce in Perth. Visitors can choose from organic and gourmet food. There is a playground for kids. The market is open every day.

Hay Street Mall

Located on the pedestrian-only Hay Street, the mall is a popular shopping area right in the heart of the Perth City. The mall has a number of branded stores although they close quite early – many around 6:00pm and do not open on weekends! There are many eateries for those who want to grab a quick bite at a reasonable price.

PERTH TRAVEL GUIDE

Harbor Town Perth

http://harbourtownperth.com.au/

Located in Wellington St, the Harbor Town Mall is easily accessible with the free yellow CAT bus service. This is the place to be for those who love to buy branded products as the mall has a number of factory outlets including Cue, Dotti, and Temt. The mall closes at 9:00pm on Fridays and by 5:30pm on all other days.

Carillon City

http://carilloncity.com.au/

Located between Hay St and Murray St, this Wi-Fi enabled mall is on the way of the yellow and red free CAT buses. Along with a number of clothing and jewelry stores, the mall has a number of fast food and Asian

PERTH TRAVEL GUIDE

cuisine outlets including Thai, Indian, and Japanese. The mall also has a number of beauty and grooming stores. Like many other malls in Perth, it is open late (8:30pm) on Fridays and closes by 5:00 pm on other days.

PERTH TRAVEL GUIDE

Know Before You Go

 Entry Requirements

With the exception of New Zealand, nationals of most countries will need a valid passport and a visa when travelling to Australia. Upon arrival, you will also be required to fill out a passenger card, which includes a declaration regarding your health and character. A tourist visa is usually valid for 6 months, but can be extended for another 6 months. If travelling to Australia for business reasons, you will want to look into the requirements for a short term or long term business visas. The former is valid for up to 3 months, while the latter is valid for up to 4 years, but requires sponsorship from an Australian company.

Health Insurance

If visiting Australia from a country that has a reciprocal health care agreement with Australia, you will be able to use Medicare - Australia's public health insurance - for the duration of your stay. Participating countries include Ireland, New Zealand,

Italy, Sweden, Norway, Slovenia, Belgium, Finland, the Netherlands and the UK. However, this only covers emergency care and limits you to using public hospitals. Visitors on a student visa from Norway, Finland, Malta and the Republic of Ireland may require additional cover and visitors who do not have access to Medicare will be required, as part of their visa application, to obtain adequate healthcare for the duration of their stay in Australia. To extend your cover, Overseas Visitors Health Cover (OVHC) can be arranged through a number of Australian health fund companies. Additional health insurance is mandatory if visiting on a long stay working visa. There are no required vaccinations for entering Australia, but a booster shot for tetanus and diphtheria will be a good idea, if your last vaccination was more than ten years ago. If travelling from Southeast Asia, you may want to get a shot for Hepatitis A and B, as well as typhoid.

Travelling with Pets

Nearly all dogs and cats travelling to Australia will need to spend some time in quarantine, but the duration depends on the country of origin. The only countries exempt from this requirement is New Zealand, Cocos Island and Norfolk Island. The minimum quarantine period is 10 days and to qualify for this, your pet will need to be tested for rabies 6 months prior to

PERTH TRAVEL GUIDE

your travel date. The cost for quarantine and customs clearance is approximately $1,800AUD. You will need to apply for an import permit for your pet. If travelling from a non-approved country such as Russia, India, Sri Lanka and the Philippines, your pet will need to spend 6 months in an approved country and be tested for rabies prior to being allowed entry in Australia. Approved countries include Antigua & Barbuda, Argentina, Austria, the Bahamas, Belgium, Bermuda, the British Virgin Islands, Brunei, Bulgaria, Canada, the Canary and Balearic Islands, the Cayman Islands, Chile, the Republic of Croatia, the Republic of Cyprus, the Czech Republic, Denmark, Finland, France, Germany, Gibraltar, Greece, Greenland, Guernsey, Hong Kong, Hungary, Ireland, the Isle of Man, Israel, Italy, Jamaica, Jersey, Kuwait, Latvia, Lithuania, Luxembourg, Macau, Malta, parts of Malaysia (Peninsular, Sabah and Sarawak only), Monaco, Montenegro, the Netherlands, Netherlands—Antilles & Aruba, Norway, Poland, Portugal, Puerto Rico, Qatar, Reunion, Saipan, Serbia, Seychelles, Slovakia, Slovenia, South Africa, South Korea, Spain, St Kitts and Nevis, St Lucia, St Vincent & the Grenadines, Sweden, Switzerland (including Liechtenstein), Taiwan, Trinidad and Tobago, the United Arab Emirates, the United Kingdom, the United States, Northern Mariana Islands, Puerto Rico and the US Virgin Islands as well as American Samoa, Bahrain, Barbados, Christmas Island, Cook Island, the Falkland Islands, the Federated States of Micronesia, Fiji,

PERTH TRAVEL GUIDE

French Polynesia, Guam, Hawaii, Iceland, Japan, Kiribati Mauritius, Nauru, New Caledonia, Niue, Palau, Papua New Guinea, Samoa, Singapore, the Solomon Islands, the Kingdom of Tonga, Tuvalu, Vanuatu and the Futuna Islands. There are quarantine stations in Sydney and Melbourne. A quarantine period can be waived in the case of service dog, provided that proper documented evidence of the dog's status is submitted, but in this case, the dog will need to be inspected upon arrival by an approved veterinarian and supervised for the 10 day period immediately after entry. You are not allowed to bring certain dog breeds such as the Dogo Argentino, Fila Brazileiro, Japanese Tosa, Pit Bull Terrier, American Pit Bull, Perro de Presa Canario or Presa Canario into Australia. Other animals that cannot be brought into Australia are chinchillas, fish, ferrets, guinea pigs, hamsters, lizards, mice, snakes, spiders and turtles. In the case of avian species, only birds originating from New Zealand are allowed.

🌐 Airports

Sydney Airport (SYD) is located just 8km south of Sydney's central business district and serves as the primary gateway for international air traffic into Australia. It is the country's busiest airport and provides connections to New Zealand, Singapore, Hong Kong, Dubai, Japan, the USA and Malaysia.

PERTH TRAVEL GUIDE

Domestically, it also provides access to the country's six main states, as well as to Tasmania. The second busiest airport is **Melbourne Airport** (MEL). It is located about 23km from the central business area of Melbourne, but this is easy to reach via the Skybus Super Shuttle, which connects to the city's public transport network at the Southern Cross station. Melbourne Airport welcomes international flights from the Far East, the Middle East and the USA and also connects to Australia's top domestic destinations. The busiest airport in Queensland is **Brisbane Airport** (BNE), which provides connections to over 40 domestic destinations and over 25 international destinations. Other important airports in Queensland are the **Gold Coast Airport** (OOL) and the **Cairns Airport** (CNS). As the 4th busiest airport, **Perth Airport** (PER) serves as a gateway to Western Australia. **Adelaide Airport** (ADL) is the most important airport in the Southern Territory of Australia, while **Darwin Airport** (DRW), one of the oldest airports in Australia, opens up the Northern Territory. **Canberra Airport** (CBR) provides access to the capital. Tasmania is served by **Hobart International Airport** (HBA) in Hobart.

🌐 Airlines

Qantas Airways is the third oldest airline in the world. It was founded in 1920 through the efforts of two Australian Flying

PERTH TRAVEL GUIDE

Corps veterans, W Hudson Fysh and Paul McGinness. The enterprise pioneered a series of milestones, starting with the establishment of an airmail service, the Flying Doctor Service, a regular connection between Brisbane and Darwin and the addition of international destinations such as Singapore. Qantas was an early adapter to the benefits of Boeing jumbo jets and one of the first airlines to establish a trans-Pacific route. Today it is Australia's national flag carrier and the country's largest airline. Qantas is a partner of the OneWorld Air Alliance, connecting it with British Airlines, Iberia, Japan Airlines, Finnair, LAN Airlines and Sri Lankan Airlines.

Qantas has a founding interest in Australia's budget service, Jetstar Airways, which is based at Melbourne Airport. Together with Qantas, Jetstar oversees Jetstar Asia Airways, Jetstar Pacific Airlines and Jetstar Japan. Qantas also operates a regional brand, QantasLink, which harnesses the combined coverage of Eastern Australian Airlines, Sunstate Airlines and Southern Australia Airlines to provide a regional and domestic service. Eastern Australia Airlines was founded late in the 1940s, when it served mainly to connect remote rural communities under the name Tamair. During the mid-1980s, it was acquired by Australian Airlines, who in turn sold it to Qantas in 1992.

PERTH TRAVEL GUIDE

After Qantas, Virgin Australia is the second largest airline. Founded under the Virgin brand by Richard Branson and Brett Godfrey in 2000, the company expanded rapidly after September 2001 to fill the gap left by the demise of Ansett Australia. Virgin Australia is in partnership with the regional service SkyWest Airlines as well as Air New Zealand and the US carrier Delta. Additionally, it operates the budget airline, Tigerair Australia as a subsidiary of Virgin Australia. Tigerair offers connections to 11 domestic destinations as well as nearby Bali.

West Wing Aviation is a domestic service based in Queensland and manages connections to smaller and more remote destinations within Queensland. Airnorth was founded in the late 1970s. Based in Darwin, it provides a regional service that covers the northern part of Australia. King Island Airlines offers connections between Moorabbin, near Melbourne and King Island, Tasmania.

 Hubs

Sydney Airport serves as the primary hub for Qantas Air. Qantas also uses Melbourne Airport, Brisbane Airport, Perth Airport and Adelaide Airport as hubs. Virgin Australia uses Brisbane Airport, Melbourne Airport and Sydney Airport as

PERTH TRAVEL GUIDE

hubs, but also has a strong presence at Adelaide Airport, Perth Airport and Gold Coast Airport. Additionally, Melbourne Airport serves as hub for the Virgin subsidiary Tigerair, as well as Jetstar Airlines. Darwin International Airport serves as a primary hub for Airnorth. West Wing Aviation uses Townsville Airport in Queensland as hub. Brisbane Airport serves as a hub for Sunstate Airlines.

Money Matters

Currency

The currency of Australia is the Australian dollar. Notes are issued in denominations of $5, $10, $20, $50 and $100. Coins are issued in denominations of 5 cents, 10 cents, 20 cents and 50 cents as well as $1 and $2.

Banking/ATMs

ATM machines are widely distributed across Australia in both urban and rural locations. Besides bank lobbies, they are often found in shopping centers, service stations, convenience stores and pubs. You should be able to use bank cards that are part of the Cirrus, Plus or Maestro networks. Most ATMs will explicitly indicate which cards are accepted. Using a debit card is fairly easy in Australia, but many ATMs will charge an additional fee of $2 or more for non-customers. There are exceptions. As the Westpac banking group is partnered with several overseas banks including Bank of America, Scotia Bank and Barclays, customers of those banks will be exempted from the banking fee. An alternative to using your bank card is the Travelex Cash Passport, an easy-to-use prepaid card which can be topped up using your debit card.

Credit Cards

MasterCard and Visa are widely accepted throughout Australia, while Diners Club and American Express will also be legal tender at larger shops and chain stores. Some shops will decline credit cards for purchases under AUS$15 and surcharges may apply for some businesses. Until recently, credit card users in Australia had the choice of using a PIN or signature as security for credit card transactions, but from August 2016, PIN-enabled cards will be mandatory. You should make sure that your credit card is compatible with this new policy. Also remember to advise your bank or credit card of your travel plans prior to your departure.

🌏 Tourist Tax

From July 2016, working backpackers will be taxed at 32.5 percent on their Australian income.

🌏 Claiming Back VAT

Visitors to Australia can obtain a refund on purchases of at least $300, spent at a single business. Residents of the Australia's External Territories - the Norfolk Islands, Christmas Island and the Cocos (Keeling) Islands - also qualify for a refund from GST paid under the Tourist Refund Scheme (TRS). To obtain a refund, you must present valid documentation of your purchases in the form of a tax invoice or sales receipt at an international airport or seaport when departing Australia and this should happen within 60 days of making those purchases. You should keep the goods handy within your hand luggage, to have it available for inspection. To save time, download the TRS app where you can enter details electronically and use a specially dedicated shortcut queue to process your claim.

PERTH TRAVEL GUIDE

🌐 Tipping Policy

In Australia, restaurants are required by law to pay their waiting staff a working wage and tipping is not really expected, although the influence of tourism as well as American culture has influenced Australian attitudes in recent years. In high-end restaurants, roughly half of the diners might be expected to leave a tip and in big cities, it will be more common to tip. If service is good and you want to show your appreciation, 10 percent is regarded as fair and sufficient. It is not common practice to tip in hotels and in casinos, tipping is forbidden. In bars, it is accepted practice to tell the bartender to keep the change. The same applies to cab drivers.

🌐 Connectivity

Mobile Phones

Australia uses the GSM mobile network, which means that it should be compatible with phones from the UK or the European Union, but may be incompatible with phones from the USA and Canada. If you are able to use Australian networks, you will still face the high charges levied for international roaming. There is an alternative. If your phone is unlocked, you will be able to replace your own SIM card with an Australian SIM card for the duration of your stay.

Australia has 3 basic mobile networks - Telstra, Vodafone and Optus. Telstra offers the best coverage of Australia's rural and more remote locations, but is also one of the more expensive operators. If you plan to stick to urban locations, the coverage offered by Optus and Vodafone might be sufficient for your needs. Telstra sim cards are available at $2, with recharge packages starting at $20. Data only packages are priced at between $30 and $50. Optus sim cards begin at $2 for just the sim, with top-ups priced at between $10 and $50. Vodafone pre-paid sim cards begin at $1 for just the sim, with data packages priced at between $3 and $15. For a super budget option, consider the deals offered by the reseller Amaysim, which also offers the option to pay for top-ups online, via PayPal.

 Dialling Code

The dialling code for Australia is +61.

PERTH TRAVEL GUIDE

🌍 Emergency Numbers

General emergency: 000

Text Emergency Relay Service: 106

MasterCard: 1800 120 113

Visa: 1800 450 346

🌍 General Information

🌍 Public Holidays

1 January: New Year's Day

26 January: Australia Day

March/April: Good Friday

March/April: Easter Monday

25 April: Anzac Day

23 June: The Queen's Birthday

25 December: Christmas

26 December: Boxing Day

There are various holidays that are celebrated at state level or within certain religious communities.

PERTH TRAVEL GUIDE

🌏 Time Zones

The Australian continent is divided into three different time zones. The eastern states of Queensland, Victoria and New South Wales, as well as the Australian Capital Territory and Tasmania fall under Australian East Standard Time (AEST), which can be calculated as Greenwich Mean Time/Co-ordinated Universal Time (GMT/UTC) +10. Australian Central Standard Time (ACST) is used in the Northern Territory, South Australia and in the town of Broken Hill, which is found in the western part of New South Wales. Australian Central Standard Time can be calculated as Greenwich Mean Time/Co-ordinated Universal Time (GMT/UTC) +9 and a half hour. Western Australia uses Australian Western Standard time, which can be calculated as Greenwich Mean Time/Co-ordinated Universal Time (GMT/UTC) +8.

🌏 Daylight Savings Time

For Daylight Savings Time, clocks are set forward by one hour at 2am on the first Sunday in October and set back one hour at 3am on the first Sunday in April. Queensland, Western Australia and the Northern Territory do not observe Daylight Savings Time.

PERTH TRAVEL GUIDE

🌏 School Holidays

In Australia, the academic year runs from January to December. Generally, schools open towards the end of January or very early in February. There is a 2 to 3 week break from the end of March or early in April, a winter vacation in June/July and a 2 week spring break in September or October. The summer vacation is usually from mid December to the end of January. Exact dates are set by the state authority in question and may vary.

🌏 Trading Hours

Trading hours are set at state rather than national level, but in most states there are little or no restrictions on hours. Generally, shopping hours in Australia are from 8am to 9pm on weekdays, 8am to 5.30pm on Saturdays and 9am to 6pm on Sundays. Most non-essential businesses will be closed on ANZAC Day, Good Friday and Christmas Day. In South Australia, trade on Sundays and Public Holidays are restricted to the hours between 11am and 5pm. In Queensland, most shopping centers close at 5pm, but will stay open for late trade one day of the week. In Western Australia, large businesses and chain stores are restricted to trading between 9am and 5pm from Monday to

Saturday and between 11am and 5pm on Sundays and Public Holidays.

🌐 Driving Policy

Australians drive on the left hand side of the road. In most states, you will be able to drive on a foreign licence, provided that it is valid and that an English translation (or International Driver's Licence) is available. The minimum driving age varies from 16 years and 6 months in the Northern Territory to 18 in Victoria, but in most states it is 17 years. The speed limit is 60km per hour for cities and urban areas, 50km per hour in suburban areas and 110km per hour on highways and rural roads. Laws regarding texting and the use of cell phones while driving vary, but in most states, a hands-free kit is required. Learner drivers or inexperienced drivers are not allowed to handle their phones at all while driving. The legal limit for drinking and driving is a Blood Alcohol Concentration (BAC) of 0.05%, but learner drivers and inexperienced drivers are not allowed to drink at all when driving.

Drinking Policy

In Australia, the minimum drinking age is 18. Children under the age of 18 are only allowed on licenced premises, if accompanied by a parent. Only businesses with a liquor licence are allowed to supply alcohol to the public and by law, they are required to ask customers and patrons for some form of identification. Local councils in Australia have the power to declare an area a dry zone, which means that no alcohol may be consumed there. The ban may relate to a particular event or can apply on an ongoing basis.

Smoking Policy

In the early 1990s, Australia introduced legislation to restrict smoking in public places. Smoking is banned in restaurants, bars and licenced clubs, although there are designated smoking areas. Recently, the ban was widened to include smoking in vehicles with children under the age of 18. Smoking is also forbidden in outdoor play areas for children, at swimming pools, bus stops and railway stations. In New South Wales, you may not smoke within 4m of a building entrance and in Western Australia, smoking is prohibited in the patrolled areas of beaches. All tobacco products are required by law to carry health warnings.

PERTH TRAVEL GUIDE

 Electricity

Electricity: 230 volts

Frequency: 50 Hz

Australia's electricity sockets are compatible with the Type I plugs, a plug that features three rectangular pins or prongs, arranged in a triangular shape, with two of the pins set at opposing angles to each other. They are similar to the plugs and sockets used in Fiji. If travelling from the USA or Canada, you will also need a power converter or transformer to convert the voltage from 230 to 110, to avoid damage to your appliances. The latest models of certain types of camcorders, cell phones and digital cameras are dual-voltage, which means that they were manufactured with a built in converter, but you will have to consult your electronics dealer about that.

Food & Drink

When they have the time for a hearty breakfast, Australians love a fry-up similar to the full English breakfast with eggs, bacon, sausage, mushroom and baked beans. Other popular breakfast options include porridge, cereal and milk or simply a slice of toast with vegemite - that is Australia's twist on good

PERTH TRAVEL GUIDE

old Marmite. Technically, Australia lies in the Orient and a robust community of Asian immigrants has ensured the enduring popularity of Asian cuisine. Australia also sometimes offers exotic game, in the form of kangaroo, emu and crocodile steak. Adventurous diners will want to sample bush food, but it is not for the faint of heart. Bush tucker originated with the hunter-gatherer lifestyle of Australia's Aboriginal people and incorporates a variety of home-grown fruits and vegetables, as well as edible seeds and insects. One of the best known delicacies is the witchetty grub, which can be eaten raw or cooked. Other indigenous staples include bush yam, bush banana, conkleberries and wattle seeds.

In Australia, beer is serious business, complete with its own lingo of buzz phrases. Australians refer to a can as a "tinnie", a case of 24 cans as a "slab" and a bottle of beer as a "brownie" or, in the case of a long-necked bottle, as a "tally". While a short-necked bottle is called a "stubby", do not mistake it with a "Darwin stubby", the Northern Territory variety with a 2.25 litre capacity. Even glasses are divided into "pints", "schooners", "middys" or "pots", according to size, and you should say "My shout" to announce your intention to buy the next round.

The most popular beer brands in Australia are VB (Victoria Bitter) and Castlemaine's XXXX Gold and other beers worth sampling include Carlton Draught, Toohey's Extra Dry, Hahn Premium Light, Crown Lager, Pure Blonde and James Boag's Premium. In Queensland and New South Wales, Bundeberg beer is another favorite. Australia has a robust wine industry, of which the best known export is Penfolds Grange. Other well established wineries are Wolf Blass, Lindemans, Rosemount, Jacob's Creek, Yalumba, Berri Estates, Yellowglen and Hardy Wine Co. Tasmania produces top notch whiskies, such as the award-winning Sullivan's Cove and great cider, such as Red Sails, Lost Pippin and Pagan Cider. When it comes to soft drinks, Coca-Cola rules. Australia's taste for coffee has been influenced by the significant community of Italian immigrants. Visiting techno-geeks can try the newly launched Smartcup, an Australian invention which can be linked to a CafePay app and lets you pay for your daily brew online.

 Useful Websites

http://www.australia.com/en
http://wikitravel.org/en/Australia
https://www.australianexplorer.com/
http://www.downundr.com/tips-and-tricks/top-ten-destinations
http://www.britz.com.au/
http://www.driveaustralia.com.au/suggested-routes/
http://ozyroadtripper.com.au/

PERTH TRAVEL GUIDE

http://australiaroadtrip.co.uk/

https://www.ozexperience.com/

Printed in Germany
by Amazon Distribution
GmbH, Leipzig